# Enki

## Sumerian God of Wisdom and Creation

# Table of Contents

# Introduction

Close your eyes and imagine traveling 6,500 years back in time. Where do you see yourself? In a cave wrapped in furs or in solid dwellings with irrigation and sanitation? When the last Ice Age happened and the glaciers receded, men became capable of farming the land,growing food, and using domesticated animals to feed themselves. They formed integrated and organized societies, and the first of these new societies happened to be in a region called Mesopotamia.

The area was home to the Sumerians, Akkadians, and Babylonians, and they were all led by kings who claimed to have a special relationship with the deities they served. They were advanced civilizations, and their deities reflected that fact. In Sumer, the god Enki was revered as the creator of mankind and worshipped by everyone who lived there. He was a mighty figure with incredible power and is believed to have ruled for over 400,000 years. Enki is a god that has been overlooked in the past, but he is worthy of your attention. He is a figurehead of a society that has remained undiscovered until 200 years ago.

The gods and rituals that define a society are often a perfect template to glimpse into how they lived. This book is all about the ancient Sumerians and how they formed a society that is still recognizable today. Enki is just one of the gods who influenced them and made their society so interesting. Welcome to a journey into the past and an introduction to one of the most influential forces of the ancient world. While the rest of the world dealt with living in the Stone Age, the ancient Sumerians started producing metal objects and building huge cities filled with factories and dwellings. The ziggurat that defended their cities were monuments to their most powerful gods and goddesses, and they reflected their importance in the lives of their citizens.

# Chapter 1:

## Who Is Enki?

In Babylonian and Akkadian mythology, the Sumerian god is a bit of an enigma known by multiple names such as Ea, Enkig, Nissiku, and Nudimmud. He is the god of love, magic, wisdom, and trickery, and his name translates as the Lord of the Earth. He is one-third of the pantheon that featured in Mesopotamia over six thousand years ago, with the other two members being Anu and Enlil. He is known for his vast appetite for sexual conquests, and he was also known as the god of semen. He had multiple incestuous relationships despite his professed desire and deep-rooted love for his wife, Ninhursag.

He is a loving and caring god who sympathizes with mankind and takes sides in disputes against the gods. His first appearance in Sumerian mythology was in 5,400 BC when shrines dedicated to him appeared in Eridu. His first appearance in Akkadian lore was dated in 2600 – 2350 BC. Other mentions are dated back to 1100 BC on a Babylonian tablet depicting the universe and the state of chaos it was in before the gods separated the fresh water and the salt water. The god Apsu rued, the male counterpart represented by the fresh water, and the goddess Tiamat rued, the salt water, the female element of the universe. When they lay together, the child of their union was born and named Enki, the Lord of the Earth.

## What Does Enki Look Like?

Enki is often depicted as a man with rivers flowing from his wide masculine shoulders that are thought to represent the rivers Euphrates and Tiger that flowed through Mesopotamia and brought life to the area. Some depictions show the rivers filled with his semen, which supports the idea that Enki was the source of all life and represented the concept of fertility and growth. Other symbols associated with fertility are the fish and the goat, which are also prominent in depictions of the god Enki.

Some images of Enki show him with a full beard and oversized hands, while others depict him living beneath the river surrounded by fish. He is often pictured with ram horns and turtles, sometimes wearing a cloak of fish scales and skin. His connection with water makes him a favorite deity for exorcists and priests and a favored deity of water diviners.

A legion of mythical creatures served Enki, and they all lived in the abzu, a vast ocean that lay beneath the Earth. He also relied on the service of a two-faced god called Isimu and seven mythical sages that Enki created to teach humans about the universe and the magical wisdom it contains. His earthly connection was with the city Eridu which housed the temple of Enki.

## The Seven Sages

Enki created the seven sages known as the Apkallu to teach mankind wisdom. They were half-man, half-fish demi-gods that emerged from the water of the Abzu, the ocean of wisdom, and were bestowed with the wisdom of sublime knowledge just like their creator Enki.

- Enmedugga, who was "allotted a good faith"
- Enmegalamma, who was "born in a house"

- Enmebuugga, who "grew up in a pastureland"
- An-Enlilda, "The conjurer of the city of Eridu"
- Utuabzu, who "ascended to heaven"

Some stories from the Sumerian mythology depict the Apkallu as malevolent creatures who performed demonic acts and were evil beings. However, some scholars believe the concept of the seven sages has appeared in so many different parts of the world that they are more likely to have resembled the watchers or sages that appeared in Greek, Chinese, Egyptian, and Indian cultures. These beings were more dedicated to teaching and sharing their wisdom rather than performing evil and bringing destruction to humankind.

Enki was also associated with a host of magical creatures, including mermaids, giants, and even demons, in his endeavors on Earth and in the heavens. He is a complex god who could be destructive or caring depending on his mood at the time. He was a healing god who brought magic and love to humanity and shared his healing chants and prayers with them in times of distress.

# Other Important Gods and Goddesses

## Tiamat, Also Known as Nammu

The goddess Tiamat was the original creation goddess who originated from the primeval water from which the universe emerged. She gave birth to the original earth, heaven, and the original gods who ruled there. Her children were Anu and Ki, the mother and father of the universe and the parents of Enki and Enlil. Some myths credit her with the creation of humans from clay, while others credit Enki with the birth of humankind.

Because she only had two children, they were destined to become spouses and siblings, and they are credited with the birth of all the following gods and goddesses. These beings were given the collective names Anunnaki which translates as the sons and daughters of Anu and Ki. In the beginning, the two gods ruled with absolute authority and were responsible for all the laws and rules that applied to the other gods. However, as time passed, they withdrew and became less prominent, allowing their offspring and descendants to become more powerful.

## Utu

The god of the sun rides his mighty chariot through the sky every day to bring light and warmth for plants to flourish. He is also the god of justice and morality, would hear the issues of both gods and mortals and apply his moral code to enforce divine justice. He is often pictured as an old man holding a serrated knife with a bright light surrounding him. Some images show him wielding a weapon that looks like a version of a pruning saw.

Utu was the twin of Inanna, the goddess who was tricked by Ereshkigal, the goddess of the underworld, and rescued by the gods in the epic tale Inanna's Descent into the Underworld. When kings reigned in the five major cities of Sumer, they would ask Utu to carve his divine rules into a slab of diorite so they could display it in their palaces and temples.

## Gula

Gula, also known as Ninkarrak, was the patron god of healers and was often invoked to heal the sick and bless surgical tools like scalpels and lancets. The doctors of Sumer would call on her to help pregnant women to give birth safely and healthily recover from the process. Gula was also responsible for using illness as a punishment for those who had wronged the god and caused distress to others. She was represented as a beautiful female surrounded by stars and would often be pictured accompanied by a dog.

# Chapter 2:

## Legends and Stories

Like all the great deities, Enki features in many stories. He is a caring god who loves his subjects and is always on hand to help them solve their problems. He is a wise god with a reputation for love and a caring attitude, and it could be said that Enki was the original "lover, not a fighter."

## The Atrahasis

In Sumerian mythology, there is a clear pattern of the younger gods being tasked with maintaining creation and seeing to the daily grind of being a god. The elder gods maintained their position of superiority and preferred eating and drinking with their elder counterparts rather than ruling. The Sumerian lore was that elders deserved respect and should be allowed to rule, while the younger gods should do the hard work. After 3,600 years of hard labor, the lesser gods rebelled and decided they didn't want to do the work anymore. The major gods, Anu – god of the sky, Enlil – god of the earth, and Enki – god of wisdom and water conferred and decided to find a way to appease the lesser gods by creating humanity to do the hard labor.

Enki created 7 men and 7 women, and they proceeded to labor for the gods, and all was well until 600 years later. The humans had proved to be incredibly fertile, and their numbers had increased into the thousands. The noise the humans made bothered the god Enlil, and he began to plan how to reduce the number of humans. He sent a plague of sickness, and the humans began to die. Enki tells them that refusing to worship the gods will help them lift the plague and ease their suffering, and the humans comply. The plague is lifted.

Another 600 years pass, and the human population has grown again, so Enlil sends famine and drought. Enki once more advises the humans on how to survive, and the drought and famine fail to destroy humanity. Enlil is outraged and plans to finally finish the humans with a mighty flood that will destroy all signs of life on Earth. Enki hears of the plan and instructs his most favored human friend Atrahasis to build an ark and fill it with pairs of animals and his own family.

Enlil sends the flood, and the Earth is ravaged so badly that the gods are overwhelmed with sadness about the loss of humanity. Even Enlil is ashamed and regretful of their actions and mourns the humans he destroyed. Eventually, Atrahasis emerges from the ark and attracts the attention of the gods. Enlil is enraged by Enki's betrayal despite his former mourning, but eventually, the pair reach an agreement. Measures are taken to ensure population levels are more controllable and that the number of people on Earth shall never be so high they will disturb the gods. Some women could not conceive, and remaining a virgin became a sign of piety to the deities. If women do produce children, demons will snatch them away, never to be seen again. The gods were appeased, and the relationship between them and humanity was restored.

## Enki and Inanna

Enki has a daughter called Inanna, and the pair ruled separate cities, Enki at Eridu and Inanna at Uruk, and were often in dispute. Enki was the holder of the rules of civilization known as the meh. He was a lusty god well known for his seduction techniques and love of women, so he had ulterior motives when he invited his daughter to a drinking contest. The pair drank copious amounts of beer and were both intoxicated. Despite his best attempts to seduce his daughter Inanna resisted and managed to keep her father at bay. Enki tried to persuade his daughter to sleep with him in his drunken state by giving her the meh as a gift. When he woke the following morning, he found the meh was gone, and all he was left with was a raging hangover and regret. He summoned demons to follow his daughter to Uruk and retrieve the meh, but she outwitted them and kept the rules of civilization. She appealed to her father to allow her to keep them and use the meh to help humanity live better. Enki, who was at heart a loving and empathetic god, realized that his daughter would use the meh for the benefit of humanity, so he allowed her to keep them.

## Enki and Ninhursag and the Creation of Life and Sickness

In Sumerian mythology, Enki has considered the creator of the universe, and his story is similar to the Garden of Eden myth in Christian terms that appear in Genesis. The story begins in a land called Dilmun, described as a Sumerian version of paradise and the land of the gods. Ninhursag, a goddess who lived there, realized that the land couldn't flourish without fresh water, and she called upon Enki, the god of water, to moisturize the land and make it more bountiful. Enki instructed the god of the sun, Utu, to rise in the sky and bring forth water from the ground.

Ninhursag was so impressed with his efforts she lay with Enki, and they had sex. This coupling represents the joining of the earth, Ninhursag, and water, Enki coming together and creating a more abundant earth. The pair were blessed with a child, and after just nine days of pregnancy, Ninhursag birthed a daughter called Ninsar, who was known as Lady Greenery and represented the arrival of plants in the land of the gods. Spring had arrived in Dilmun.

Ninsar reaches adulthood in just nine days, and Enki spies her by the riverbed and seduces her (in some versions of the story, he rapes her), and she falls pregnant. As is the norm in Dilmun, after nine days, she gives birth to a daughter Uttu who reaches adulthood in a further nine days. She is the spider goddess of weaving who weaves webs to interconnect all the plants, and her eight legs represent forms of life spreading around the land.

Ninhursag has now had enough of Enki and his lustful ways, and she warns Uttu that her grandfather will soon be seeking her out for sex. Enki approaches Uttu and asks the goddess if he can do anything that will make him more attractive to her. She asks the god to bring cucumber, apples, and grapes to her so she can taste the fruit. The fruit has phallic connotations, and Enki is encouraged by her request. He brings the fruit to her and expects to be rewarded, but Uttu tells him she isn't going to sleep with him. He rapes her and leaves her in distress and alone. Worried she will give birth to her grandfather's baby, she goes to Ninhursag and asks the goddess for her help. Ninhursag removes all traces of semen from Uttu and casts it into the dirt. Nine days later, eight magnificent plants appear in the dirt; the alfalfa, honey, atutu, actaltal, du, anharu, trcc, and vegetable plants are the first plants to be created.

Enki is unaware of these new creations, and when he spies them from his boat, he asks his companion

Isimud to investigate. When he returns from Dilmun, he tells Enki the new plant's names and that they have originated from his seed. Enki eats the plants and finds them delicious, but his actions anger Ninhursag. She leaves Dilmun and abandons Enki, which leads to him falling ill and beginning to die. The rest of the gods are helpless and cannot save Enki; his only hope is for the absent Ninhursag to return and nurse him back to help.

The gods send a sneaky fox to be the intermediary between Enki and Ninhursag, and it volunteers to take the earth goddess back to Dilmun to help the dying god. She is remorseful about leaving him and welcomes the dying god to rest beside her vagina. She kisses Enkil and asks him where his pan is. As the dying god responds to her questions, she takes that pain away and gives birth to another god. The Earth Mother repeats the process eight times and creates eight new gods to join the existing deities of Sumer.

## The Uniter of Languages

Jay Crisostomo, a renowned translation professor at the University of Michigan, translated a Sumerian epic in 2019 that told Enki's tale and the part he played in creating a universal language. He advises the kings of the lands and implores them to embrace the language of the gods, i.e., Sumerian, and become more united and powerful.

Enki appears in multiple myths in Sumerian legends and is undoubtedly a major influence. His offspring and relationships are prevalent in historical events, and the city of Eridu was considered sacred.

## The Connection to Christianity

While many differences exist between Sumerian and Christian stories, some similarities cannot be ignored. They share a similar creation story leading to a comparison between Enkil and Ninhursag and Adam and Eve. Both religions talk about the creation of human beings and plants, but they don't have detailed descriptions of how animals were created. Both religions show humans as superior beings and give them power over the other beings on Earth, but they also expect humans to offer sacrifices and offerings to the gods.

The great flood is mentioned in both religions and is a purge of the Earth by gods to rid the world of humans. In Christianity, God, the supreme being, creates an ark and saves humans and animals from destruction. At the same time, in Sumerian mythology, it is Enkil working against his fellow gods. Could it be that Sumerian mythology had influences on Christian teachings? It would seem so; surely, the stories are too similar to be a coincidence.

The king's list is another example of similarities to the Bible. It has a list of pre- and post-flood kings, appearing to show impressive lifespans before the flood yet regular spans after the flood. In the Bible, the kings that ruled before Noah also had lifespans that covered thousands of years, yet the rulers after Noah had shorter spans that reflected actual human life expectancy. Both lists had eight rulers pre-flood and had similarities between their lives that linked the king's list with Genesis.

# Chapter 3:

## Enki's Lineage

Like most gods and goddesses, Enki has an extended family, and his parents and children are featured in ancient Sumerian tales. His parents were around for the creation of the universe and played a significant part in the legends surrounding the Sumerian belief system.

## Meet the Parents

### Anu

Anu is the father of Enki, and his name means "sky god." His parents were Anshar and Kishar, who represented heaven and earth. Although he features in many myths and tales, he was often a background character despite his position as the lord of the sky. As his veneration grew, so did the distance between Anu and the lesser gods. He became a minor player in some of the most well-known myths of the time, including the epic of Gilgamesh, the myth of Adapa, and Enuma Elish.

Anu was a benevolent god who eventually withdrew from other gods and humanity and retreated higher into the heavens as a master creator, but he was still venerated on Earth. A temple in the city of Uruk was dedicated to his name and used as an astronomical observatory and library between 2000 BC and 150 BC. Even though he wasn't associated with the daily lives of man, he continued to receive offerings from the people who visited the temple. His roles were considered to be the "chairman of the board" and Heavens great patriarch who controlled the meh even though Enki was the keeper of the laws of the universe.

## Nammu

Mother of the god Enki, Nammu was a goddess associated with water and protective magic. She had the power to deflect evil and dispel harmful influences and apotropaic observances. She appears in the text as a creative goddess and the spouse of Anu, but there is very little information about her character or importance in Sumer at that time. A stone was discovered indicating a temple of Nammu was constructed in an area known as Sealand. It was dedicated to the blessings and worship of the goddess.

## Ninhursag

The wife of Enki Ninhursag was an important and influential figure in Sumerian mythology. She was his one true love despite his philandering ways. Ninhursag was married to a minor god named Sul-pa-e, with whom she had three children, but her marriage to Enki is the union that appears more frequently in Sumerian legends. Her symbol is the Greek Omega accompanied by a knife, which is thought to represent the uterus and the blade used to cut the umbilical cord, strengthening her representation as the Mother goddess and the Queen of the Birthing Hut. She is often depicted suckling an infant to her breast or crying over the death of her beloved children (humanity) following disasters. It is reported that she suckled kings to her left breast, which represents feminine light and energy. She was honored by many temples across Mesopotamia for thousands of years.

# The Children of Enki and Ninhursag

**Asarluhi** – The god of magical knowledge and the patron deity of Kuara. He created incantations to heal the sick and often acted as an intermediary between mankind and Enki.

**Enbilulu** – The god of dikes and canals, is associated with irrigation and was also given powers over Euphrates and Tigris rivers by his father. He is also attributed to the creation of weeks, days, and months alongside the moon god Nanna.

**Adapa** – The human sage who unwittingly refused the gift of immorality in the tale known as "Adapa and the South Wind." He was an important figure in Sumerian times and was regarded as a wise leader who brought power to exorcisms and other religious activities. He is a mortal man who was given the power of wisdom by his mother and father and whose name was often used in incantations and rituals to invoke wisdom and the power of knowledge.

**Marduk** – The god of magical knowledge, who was the patron of the city of Babylon and was associated with Utu, the sun god. He is associated with the planet Jupiter, and his symbol is the snake dragon and spade.

In the story of Enki and Ninhursag, more children were created when Ninhursag took Enki's pain and transformed it into physical beings. These children were all given healing powers and had separate associations that formed the earthly elements that were so important to humankind.

The eight offspring were:

1. **Abu** – The god of plants who was considered a lesser god and didn't feature in many tales in Sumerian mythology. He was married to Gula, but the pair failed to make an impression.

2. **Ninti** – The goddess and giver of life. Ninti featured heavily in Sumerian mythology and appeared in some of the early texts found in Lagash. Her temples were also found in the city, and she is referred to as Ninti, the mother; Ninti, the crown; and Ninti, the mistress of life.

3. **Emshag** – God of fertility who was rarely featured in mythology. His powers were

overshadowed by those of his father, who was the original and most powerful source of fertility.

4. **Azimua** – The goddess of healing who was worshipped and had a temple in Umma.

5. **Nintulla** – The god of precious metals was assigned power over the region Magan which is now known as the United Arab Emirates in modern-day geography. It was rich in copper and diorite and was a wealthy area of Sumer.

6. **Nanshe** – The goddess of divination, dream interpretation, and fertility. She was associated with birds and fish and the marshlands. She was associated with social justice, and she completed certain administrative tasks such as weighing and measuring the character of humankind and would often intervene to help widows and orphans. Her sense of justice meant she became known as the protective goddess who guarded people and buildings against harm.

7. **Ninkasi** – The goddess of beer. She is associated with both the positive and negative

aspects of drinking beer and was also known as "the lady who fills the mouth." Although she was a minor deity, she was popular with the Sumerians because of their love of beer and was known as "the divine barmaid."

8. **Ninsitu** – The goddess of healing who was also known as the "goddess who raised the dead." Her appearance in ancient texts describes her in a physician's role, and she is often pictured with a dog, as the ancient Sumerians believed that the healing properties of a dog's saliva were incredibly powerful.

## Other Associates of Enki

Enlil was Enki's twin brother and the god of air and wind. His primary city of worship was Nippur, and his temple was called the Ekur. Enlil was the favorite son of ancient Sumer and the only god with direct access to Anu, his father. As the influence of Anu waned, Enlil became more prominent and was regarded as the keeper of the Tablets of Destiny. The tablets were stolen from Enlil by a giant monstrous bird called Anzu, who hated Enlil and envied his power. Despite his best efforts, Enlil could not retrieve these tablets, and all the gods and heroes he sent to get them returned empty-handed. His son Ninurta finally conquers the giant bird, restores the tablets to their original source, and establishes Enlil's position as the chief ruler of the Sumerian pantheon.

Enlil is credited as the inventor of the pickaxe, a valuable tool in Sumerian legend. His original pickaxe was made from pure gold and had a lapis lazuli head. He used the tool to teach humans how to cultivate the land, pull out weeds and grow plants, and build on that concept to create magnificent cities for themselves and their families. Enlil is credited with the ability to form societies and teach humans how to live alongside each other in harmony.

Other qualities of Enlil include being a successful arbitrator, and he was often pictured in the role of a judge. Quarrels and disputes were brought to him, and he would settle them. Enil established a hierarchy among the gods and created two powerful forces known as Enten and Emesh, a shepherd and a farmer who were tasked with teaching abundance to humanity and encouraging them to flourish and become a successful civilization. When the two gods argued and fell out when Emesh tried to claim Enten's position and power, Enlil intervenes and restores harmony so the pair can resume their original positions and rule successfully.

## Enlil and Ninlil

Enlil is featured in one of the most epic tales of love between a god and goddess. Enlil falls in love with Ninlil, and she is equally enamored of the young god. However, Ninlil's mother is firmly against the union. One day Enil follows Ninlil to the river where she is planning to bathe, and the pair consummate the union. Ninlil falls pregnant and gives birth to the moon god Nanna.

The gods are furious at the young god for going against Ninlil's mother, and they banish him from Nippur to Kur, the ancient Sumerian land of the netherworld. Ninlil is heartbroken, and she travels to Kur to look for her mate and bring him back to Nippur so they can live together despite her mother's wishes. Enlil knows he can't allow her to succeed in her quest, as the gods would punish both of them, but he still wants to be with his true love. He disguises himself as the keeper of the gates to Kur, and when Ninlil attempts to enter, he seduces her, and the pair eventually have three more children together despite being kept apart.

The moral of the story is that true love conquers all, and it highlights Enlil's stance as the god of the family, and he was worshipped as such. They set a precedent that love defies all laws, and even when one partner is banished to Kur, they find a way to be together.

When Marduk, the son of Enki, became the new king of the gods, Enlil remained a firm favorite among the ancient Sumerians. His father, Anu, and Enlil willingly handed over the majority of power to Marduk and encouraged the young god to rule.

# Chapter 4:

## The Sumerian Underworld

It is important to understand how the Sumerians worshipped and revered their gods, but it is also important to understand what was happening in the Underworld while the gods ruled from heaven. Most religions and beliefs have some form of an afterlife or a place where souls can reside when they leave the physical plane. This type of myth is as old as time itself and validates the human belief in good and evil. As part of the Sumerian and Mesopotamian cosmology, the Underworld was a subterranean plane that was ruled by a feared and respected female deity. This in itself is unusual, women were mostly associated with nurturing and family ties, and not many goddesses were associated with the afterlife.

In Sumerian beliefs, all souls went to the Underworld, a place known as Kur or Irkalla and the realm of the dead. All human souls go there, but it also has a section to house the gods who have displeased their elders and broken the rules. Kur is described as a vast cosmopolitan metropolis with temples, palaces, and other residential buildings. Kir resembles the cities on Earth but is subterranean and ruled by a mighty female goddess Ereshkigal. Her name translates as "Queen of Great Below" or the "Lady of the Great Palace." She employs supernatural beings called Galla, seven mighty demons who sat naked on her lap when she was on her throne.

When other souls entered Kur, they were destined never to leave, but the Galla were different. They could leave Kur and roam the earth to terrorize mortals and drag them back to the Underworld. They were mentioned in an ancient Sumerian poem that told of beings that "touched no food, drank no water, and didn't taste the sacred flour or drink the sacred wine." The poem described beings who hated children and were intent on taking them from their parents and transporting them to Kur.

## The Goddess Ereshkigal

Some tales say that Ereshkigal is Anu's daughter, created from his salty tears at the loss of a lover.

Others myths say she was the daughter of Nanna, the god of the moon, and Ningal, the goddess of the reeds. They both agree that Kur was a gloomy and dank place where the dead drank water from muddy puddles and ate dust as their food.

She became the goddess of the Underworld when a dragon named Kur abducted her and brought her to his realm, also called Kur. The gods and goddesses sent to rescue her never returned, and they, too, were consigned to the depths of Kur for eternity. Even gods were able to return from the dead. However, when Ereshkigal's sister, Inanna, the goddess of heaven, decided to visit her sister and observe the funeral rites for her dead husband, it was agreed she would be able to leave following the ceremony. As Inanna passed through the seven gates that led to the inner sanctum of Kur, she was asked by the gatekeeper Neti to remove an item of clothing.

Unbeknownst to Inanna, her sister had instructed the gatekeeper to take a piece of clothing or jewelry at every stage to leave her sister naked and vulnerable when she reached the throne room where her sister sat. The Annuna of the dead gathered in the room and passed judgment on the hapless goddess, leading to her death. Her sister Ereshkigal brutally killed her, and her naked, bloody corpse was hung on the wall by a hook for all to see. The gods were incensed at the trickery and subsequent death of one of the most powerful goddesses, and they descended to Kur in droves and managed to revive Inanna and take her back to the heavens to resume her role as the goddess of the heavens.

## Marriage and the Underworld

Being the goddess of the Underworld didn't interfere with Ereshkigal's love life, as she married four husbands. However, her most celebrated marriage was her last, and her husband was Nergal, the god of death and pestilence. The gods were having a feast in the heavens, and they asked Ereshkigal if she wanted to attend, but as the queen of the Underworld, she could not leave the realm of the dead. So, she sent her representative Namtar. When her envoy arrived, the majority of the gods treated her with respect and showed her the same deference they would have shown Ereshkigal. The one god who refused to acknowledge Namtar was Nergal, who was incredibly rude and disrespectful to the envoy and ignored protocol.

When Namtar returned to Kur, she told the goddess how she had been treated, and Ereshkigal was so angry with the reception Nergal had given her representative and summoned the god to visit her in Kur and explain himself. Her original plan is to kill Nergal for his disrespect, but what happens next differs in the two main versions of the story. In the first version, she seduces Nergal, and he stays in Kur for six days as her lover before he returns to the world of the living. Ereshkigal is distraught and pining for her new lover, and she demands that he returns to her side. Nergal has developed feelings for the goddess, and he agrees to return and live as her husband and king, sharing the power equally and reigning as the Sumerian version of a power couple.

In the alternative version, Nergal travels to the Underworld prepared to kill the goddess, and when he arrives in Kur, he brutally drags her from her throne and is poised to kill her. Ereshkigal pleads with him to spare her life and agrees that if he does, she will share her life and power with him by agreeing to become his wife. Whichever version you prefer, they both have the same ending; the two deities marry and share the power of the Underworld for eternity.

All stories of the Underworld show the respect the ancient Sumerians placed on death and the world of the dead. The rules governing the Underworld were also applied to the land of the living. Ereshkigal may have been destined to remain in her domain, but her influence went far beyond her land. She was widely recognized as a force of nature even in the land of the living. The power she wields is more impressive than even the most powerful gods or goddesses that rule the heavens. Death is inevitable, and even when they are cheated, there are still rules to follow.

## Sumerian Ghosts and Their Role in the Underworld

While most souls were destined to spend eternity in Kur, there were exceptions. Because the food and drink in the Underworld were so disgusting, the living would often leave offerings at the gravesides of the loved ones who had passed over. The dead would be allowed to visit the land of the living briefly to collect the offerings and bring them back to the Underworld for their comfort. Once the offerings stopped, the souls would then be damned and condemned to an eternity of dirt and muddy water.

Other circumstances include issues with a person's death and would allow their souls to return to earth and put their issues right so they could return to the Underworld. If the deceased person had been buried improperly or hadn't been given a decent sendoff, they could return to earth and demand that their bodies be buried correctly. If they were the victim of a criminal or unnatural death, Ereshkigal would grant them the right to avenge their death and put matters right.

Because the reasons for their return were often vengeful, ghosts were regarded as unpleasant beings who weren't welcome in the land of the living. They would return and possess the bodies of their friends or relatives, or they would appear as apparitions. It was believed that when a ghost possessed the body of a living being, it entered through the ears, so if a person started to experience ringing in their ears or sharp pain, one possibility could be they were experiencing possession by a ghost.

## Getting Rid of Ghosts Sumerian Style

The only surefire way to get rid of ghosts would be to put their issues right and allow them to return to the Underworld as part of the natural process. The Sumerians had trained doctors who were sent to interview the possessed or people plagued by an apparition about why they thought the ghosts had returned to haunt them. They would be questioned about any offenses or wrongs they may have committed that could have triggered the haunting. Ideally, that would lead to the ghost leaving with a sense of resolve.

If the issues couldn't be resolved, the other option would be exorcism to get rid of the ghost. The Sumerian god Shamash was the god of justice and would visit Kur each evening to judge the dead and listen to their pleas to return to the earth. The living also invoked him to help them pacify or restrain ghosts that had risen from the Underworld. Some ghosts would trick the gods and return to earth for no real reason so they could haunt the living and cause terror and fear just because they could.

These ghosts were always dealt with harshly and returned to Kur in disgrace. They would be stripped of any privileges, and any offerings left by their relatives would be taken from them and distributed among the dead who had no living relatives to leave offerings. If the ghost had returned to cause havoc for no reason, the exorcism would be a simple process and extremely effective, but if the issues were real, the process would have been more complicated.

The idea that souls in the Underworld still had issues to resolve and had a genuine reason for returning from the dead is a common theme in many cultures. Greece, China, and many other belief systems had ways for the spirits to return and put matters right. The Sumerian Underworld existed to remind the living to care for their dead relatives with offerings and remember them even after their death. Cultures that believed in possession also allowed people to blame sickness and illness on the spirits when they couldn't find medical reasons for their ailments.

# Chapter 5:

## Who Were the Sumerians?

The ancient Sumerians are still a mystery to historians. However, some facts about them have surfaced and helped us understand more about these sophisticated people and how they lived and worshipped. Their society originated in the fourth millennium BC and consisted of around a dozen states or cities that lay between the Tigris and the Euphrates and harnessed the silt-laden waters to farm. The oldest and most populated city was called Uruk, and at the peak of its success, it housed over 60,000 people. In the year 2,800 BC, it was the biggest city in the world.

Sumerians constructed their homes from marsh reeds and mud bricks and were connected by sophisticated irrigation canals to form the earliest form of sanitation and cleansing. Defensive walls surrounded the cities and were often dominated by ziggurats that formed pyramid-like temples where the ancient Sumerians would gather to worship the god Enki and his contemporaries.

## Girl Power: Sumerian Style

Just as the goddess Inanna was a major part of the deities of the period, it is also reported that a female ruler is listed on the famous "Kings list," one of the most important artifacts from the era. The clay tablet lists the kings of the time and how long they reigned. The information listed on the tablet is a strange blend of fact and fiction and lists a king who purportedly lived for 43,200 years. The female ruler is listed as Kubaba, a female innkeeper who rose to power in the city of Kish around 2,500 BC. She reportedly seized power by bribing a fisherman to offer his catch to the god Marduk at the temple of Esagil. The god welcomed her offerings, and he "entrusted Kubaba, the keeper of the tavern, the sovereignty of the whole world."

That's right, her campaign for sovereignty worked because she offered the god fish and beer from her tavern. Sumerians were especially fond of beer made from bread and water, so the path from tavern keeper to queen wasn't as unusual as it first seemed. Kubaba would have been highly respected, and she would have been regarded as a successful businesswoman with connections to spiritual and divine beings. Whatever the reasons for her reign, she was successful and is credited with making a "firm foundation for the city of Kish," and her legacy lasted for over a century. Even after her death, she retained a divine association, and her legacy evolved into the entity Cybele, the Greek-Roman goddess known as the "great mother of the gods," not a bad legacy for a bartender!

## They Developed Cuneiform Writing

Back in 3,400 BC, the ancient Sumerians developed a form of writing that was the first sophisticated method of recording data and information. They used several hundred characters and inscribed the information into wet clay tablets with reed stylus, then left them to harden in the sun. The earliest tablets were dedicated to rather mundane subjects like accounts and recording business transactions, but as writing developed, it began to blossom. Later tablets contained poetry and literature and recorded historical events. Over time the script used by the ancient

Sumerians would form the basis for many cultural texts and multiple languages. Archaeologists found evidence that cuneiform text was still being used 4,500 years later in the region referred to as the Nera East that covers the Ottoman Empire.

## Sumerians Traveled Extensively

Because their homeland was devoid of key materials like timber and stone, the ancient Sumerians had to think of other ways to gain access to these important resources. They traveled to the island of Dilmun, the area known as Bahrain in the present day, to trade silver and barley for copper. The ancient Sumerians loved lapis lazuli, incorporated it into art and jewelry, and traveled to Afghanistan to get it. They would undertake journeys that lasted for months to Turkey and Lebanon to gain access to cedar wood and precious metals. Sumerians were the first commercial traders, forming history's earliest trade networks.

## Their Culture and History Were Lost Until the 19th Century

Mesopotamia and Sumer lost their cultural identity when the Amorites and Babylonians occupied the lands in 2,000 BC, and their history became lost in the annals of time. They became a forgotten society, and all records of their history, language, and even their names were buried beneath the sands of the Iranian deserts for millennia. Archaeologists eventually found evidence of their existence in the 19th century when they discovered Sumerian artifacts whilst hunting for evidence of the existence of the ancient Assyrians. The French and British teams found evidence of the ancient Sumerian lives, and they assigned scholars to decipher the language on the clay tablets they found beneath the desert sands.

Since the first excavation, archaeologists have unearthed numerous pieces of pottery, artworks, sculptures, and close to half a million clay tablets, most of which are still awaiting translation.

## Other Noteworthy Facts about the Ancient Sumerians

The ancient Sumerians were an inventive bunch, and they were the forerunners of many mass-produced items as they created new technologies for large-scale production. Because their homeland had very few natural resources, they needed to find ways to transform mundane materials into spectacular items. They had a lot of clay, and they used it well. It became their version of what we call plastic, and they used it to form items for trade and improve their people's everyday lives.

They soon recognized the benefit of being organized and transformed their production methods so they could think big and be more innovative. The texts and writings they left suggest that their society admired ambition and success and rewarded it with honor and recognition. The Sumerians knew the power of development, and some of their inventions are still used today.

## The Potter's Wheel

Other civilizations were producing pots, but generally, pottery was only found in wealthier households. The Sumerians developed a wheel that allowed mass production, and early pots were used to contain workers' rations, much like the plastic Tupperware we use today.

## The Chariot

While the Sumerians didn't invent the wheel, they did something very clever with the original design.

They turned the idea of the wheel into a vehicle with just two wheels powered by a team of animals. There is evidence that the chariot was in use in the 3000s BC in Sumer and was probably used for military use and ceremonial occasions. They may have used them for transportation in the country, but it would have made any journey rough and difficult.

## The Plow

There is solid evidence that the Sumerians invented the first plow as a manual was found during excavations that gave detailed instructions on using various types of plows from the era. They also specified that any users of the plows should pay homage to the goddess Ninkilim, the goddess of fieldmice, to prevent the grain from being eaten by rodents.

## Textile Mills

Other cultures were producing cloth from wool, but individuals did the process. The Sumerians soon realized that clothing was a valuable commodity and could be used for trade. They turned their temples into huge factories that mass-produced cloth by crossing kin lines to weave the wool faster.

## Bricks

The lack of timber and stone for building meant the Sumerians had to use the materials they had to hand to create successful dwellings. They weren't the only society to use clay for building structures; they were the first to create molds for producing bricks in large amounts. They developed the art of brickmaking and used them to create large cities filled with clay dwellings.

## Metallurgy

The Sumerians traded with Dilmun for copper and soon developed ways of working with metal that were far more advanced than other cultures of the era. They created furnaces where they burned reeds and a method of controlling temperatures using bellows that could be worked with the feet or hands. They created impressive artworks with the meta that depicted animals and birds in detail, but their most impressive work was more practical. Chisels, razors, and other metal items could be used In the home or as a weapon.

## Mathematics

Ever since man evolved, there has been a need to keep track of numbers. The primitive societies used notches on bones, but the Sumerians became the first society to develop mathematics. They created a formal numbering system that worked with units of 60 and became the basis of the calculations still used today.

# Chapter 6:

## Eridu: The Original City

I t would be impossible to understand the god Enki without studying the city most associated with him, Eridu. It is allegedly one of the first five cities ever built in the world and the heart of the region before the Deluge or the Great Flood changed the world. The site of Eridu was discovered in 1854 a couple of miles south of Moghair, the ancient city of Ur, and in the center of an arid dry bed that once housed an inland sea. The locals called it Abu Sharein, and the whole area was classed as a ruin.

Eridu is believed to have housed the original Tower of Babel and was the home of the largest city following the Great Flood. It is believed the Tower of Babel wasn't meant to worship the gods but was instead a testament to the glory of man. It celebrated the unification of the people and their sharing of a single language so that communications were clear and concise. It is part of Christian beliefs that this angered God, and he came down from heaven and scattered them to different lands to confuse them and punish them for their vanity.

The location of Eridu today is in Iraq and is better known as Abu Sharein, the name the original locals had bestowed on it. The archaeologists who discovered the city were amazed at the sheer size of the structures. It seemed inconceivable that such a random site once housed one of the most important cities in the world.

## The Ziggurats of Eridu

During the following 200 years, many structures were discovered at the site, providing historians with more insight into how the city functioned and how the ancient Sumerians lived and worshipped. There have been successive temples found in the city, and the temple of Enki the temple was found to have housed a holy tree in a holy grove. Texts from the era describe the king of the city as performing his rites and blessings in the grove and dedicating them to the god Enki, the master gardener of the heavens.

Other temples were found in the form of ziggurats, huge, stepped pyramids with successively receding levels. Worshippers would visit the complex and choose to offer their gifts to the gods in smaller rooms with dedicated offering tables. The ziggurats weren't just places of worship; they were important places for people to meet and share their lives. If the citizens of Eridu had a dispute, they would bring it to the temple and ask for intervention and advice from the gods and the holy men. They would sit with their neighbors and share food and drink.

## The Eridu Genesis

Beyond the architectural remains of the city, there is very little information about Eridu except the Sumerian text known as the Eridu Genesis. The oldest Sumerian epic was discovered in 1893 and is related to the story of the flood and the epic of Glagaash. Unfortunately, the tablets the text was written on were badly damaged, and only a third of the text is legible.

The story starts with the creation of the world and its population of "black-headed people" (the Sumerians) and their animals. It tells of the pantheon of gods, Anu, Enki, Enlil, and of the wife of

Enki, Ninhursag, who were the creators of cities, and how Enki, the patron of Eridu was the mightiest of all. It has patchy accounts of the flood and the gods' disputes over humankind's fate, but the narrative does cover the truce the gods made to keep humanity safe. It is considered the first written account of the popular myth surrounding the flood, which has appeared in numerous cultures across the ancient world. Some experts believe this proves that an actual physical flood must have happened and that the different cultures equated the event with the creation of the world.

Other scholars disagree and attribute the tale's popularity to traveling tradesmen spreading the word of the flood and how it was an attempt to rid the earth of humanity. It is believed that the Sumerian version was the original tale, and that fueled travelers' tales for millennia as they traveled the great caravan routes of Western Asia. Each version of the story contains the same concept: God's wrath, the decision to send a flood to cleanse the earth, and then the regret of their decision. In the Christian version, God even sends a rainbow to signify his promise never to try and eradicate humanity again.

In each version, the moral is the same, be mindful of the divine presence in your lives and maintain the goodwill of the gods or suffer the consequences.

## The Incantation of Eridu

There is plenty of evidence about how vast the city of Eridu was, but other texts connect it closely to Sumerian magic and myths that singled it out as a city filled with spiritual energy and magic. When the god Marduk rose to power, he connected with the city through his fathers' ties. Enki was already the patron deity, and his son Marduk strengthened these connections and made the city a source of power for his own personal form of magic known as Mardukite magic which still has followers today.

These writings were especially important to historians as they described the Incantation of Eridu, which was a magical ritual designed to compel the gods to follow the teachings of Marduk. Practitioners used these incantations to create magical hierarchies and give individuals god-like powers. During a ceremony or religious procedure, the person seeking to connect with the god Marduk would invoke him with incantations and other rituals to become the god in human form. The procedure is similar to the Catholic ritual of a priest taking on the form of Christ to imitate and reenact the Last Supper and be Christ's representative on earth.

Despite the city being mostly sand dunes and ruins today, it remains a spiritual and fascinating place to visit. It was a magnificent place and a unique city of its time, and visitors can still feel the spirits and energy from those times.

# Chapter 7:

## Where Are Sumerian Relics Found Today?

We already know that the existence of the Sumerian race and culture was only discovered in the 19th century, but the relics the archaeologists uncovered have provided a steady stream of information about their skills and artistic talents. We have already covered some of their more impressive achievements, but if you have developed a taste for Sumerian life and want to see the actual objects found at the sites, there are multiple options to choose from.

In the wonderful world we live in today, there are numerous options to see Sumerian art and relics online, and the website Sumerian Shakespeare is a great place to start. You can see the tablets that contained early cuneiform writing and study their translations. There are artists' impressions of some of the magnificent structures built to worship the gods and detailed reconstructions of the mighty cities that formed in the fertile crescent that was the land of the Sumerians.

Visiting the area isn't always an option for tourists, so you can experience what the city of Eridu and Ur looked like and what the citizens did every day. You can experience the forts civilization from the comfort of your own home and marvel at the artistic representations of the gods and goddesses and how they were worshipped.

The site also includes detailed maps that show conflicts among the cities and the wars they fought to survive. It has pictures of weapons and armor from the era that show how superior the Sumerian army actually was. Sumerian life was fascinating, and although they got a lot of things right, they were also a flawed bunch. They were the first civilization that created a ruling class, and there was a distinct disparity in income distribution, leading to greed and enslavement for those who didn't conform.

If you do want to experience Sumerian art and treasures in person, perhaps the best places to visit are the McClung Museum in Knoxville, Tennessee, the Pennsylvania Museum, or the British Museum in London. They all have extensive exhibits representing the Sumerian civilization and multiple tablets from the era. The excavation of the Royal Cemetery in Ur was as important as the Tomb of Tutankhamun in archaeological terms and contained relics from 16 royal tombs and over 1700 tombs of "ordinary" people. In the pit of Queen Puabi, they discovered ornate jewelry and clothing made from precious metals and lapis lazuli. The tomb also contained a wooden lyre that was decorated with the head of a bull and depictions of animals drinking and performing in an original gold plaque.

These treasures do sometimes travel and visit other museums, so check what is happening and where you can visit them. The trip to see these amazing treasures is well worth the effort and is every bit as impressive as anything from the Egyptian tombs.

# Conclusion

Welcome back from the birth of civilization! How was the trip? There is a lot of interest in other civilizations and mythology today, and the emergence of the Viking gods and other deities like Thor and Odin dominate the media. The films and tv series they inspire are all remarkably interesting, but why stop there? Aren't the tales from Sumerian and Mesopotamian times just as exciting and filled with heroes and villains? Surely a mythology with a bad-ass female ruler of the underworld would make great content for entertainment.

The Sumerian era is packed with tales of amazing feats of bravery and gods and goddesses fighting and making love. More remarkably, they all existed in a time when civilization as we know it was just emerging, so their tales became even more significant. If you are growing tired of traditional stories of gods and goddesses, then the Sumerian era is packed with less well-known deities that are original and have their own backstories. The beauty of this era is that each god and goddess have multiple personalities depending on who recorded their stories, so you can read the same myth in several different forms. It's like having access to your favorite book, but it is written by different authors who have all put their own twist on the content.

The sands of the Iranian desert may have hidden Sumer and Sumerians for centuries, but now they are here to tell their tales in detail. The exciting fact is that thousands of tablets remain untranslated, so who knows what they contain? More myths and exciting facts about people who lived over five thousand years ago could soon be uncovered. Sumerian mythology is the gift that just keeps giving, and you can be the recipient of that gift.

Thanks for reading the book and being part of the magical trip back to a time when man was beginning to live in communities that resemble the civilization we know today.

# References


Andrews, Evan. "9 Things You May Not Know about the Ancient Sumerians." HISTORY, 5 Feb. 2019, www.history.com/news/9-things-you-may-not-know-about-the-ancient-sumerians.

Dhar, Rittika. Enki and Enlil: The Two Most Important Mesopotamian Gods | History Cooperative. 2 June 2022, historycooperative.org/enki-and-enlil/.

dhwty. "Ereshkigal: The Mighty Mesopotamian Goddess of the Underworld." Www.ancient-Origins.net, www.ancient-origins.net/myths-legends-europe/ereshkigal-mighty-mesopotamian-goddess-underworld-0010004.

"Enki (Ea) - Sumerian God of Water, Creation, and Fertility." Mythology.net, 28 May 2017, mythology.net/others/gods/enki/.

"Enki and Ninhursag and the Creation of Life and Sickness." JB's Modes of Knowledge Wiki, jabibbles. fandom.com/wiki/Enki_and_Ninhursag_and_ the_Creation_of_Life_and_Sickness.

"Eridu Genesis." World History Encyclopedia, www.worldhistory.org/Eridu_Genesis/.

"Goddess Ereshkigal: The First Ruler of the Underworld." TheCollector, 4 Apr. 2022, www. thecollector.com/goddess-ereshkigal/.

Hardy, James. "The 10 Most Important Sumerian Gods | History Cooperative." History Cooperative, 22 Apr. 2022, historycooperative.org/sumerian-gods/.

Kiger, Patrick J. "9 Ancient Sumerian Inventions That Changed the World." HISTORY, Aug. 2019, www.history.com/news/sumerians-inventions-mesopotamia.

"Who Was the Sumerian God Enki?" Gaia, www. gaia.com/article/who-was-sumerian-god-enki.

9 7 9 8 2 1 5 8 5 9 1 6 2